Victoria

The ART of CORRESPONDENCE

Victoria

The ART of CORRESPONDENCE

FROM THE EDITORS OF *VICTORIA*

83 press

Hoffman Media
2323 2nd Avenue North
Birmingham, AL 35203
hoffmanmedia.com

ISBN 979-8-9874820-5-6
Printed in China

83 press

R
's GRAVENHAGE
Willem de Zwijgerlaan
Gv. Wz.
No 169
HONOR
UNITED STATES POSTAGE
3 CENTS 3
U. S.
SEP 7
1945
NAVY

CONTENTS

- Jane
I must learn to be content
ith being happier than I deserve.
- Jane Austen
ve.
I must
to be content
with
with being
than I deserve.
- Jane Austen
tent
I deserve.
I must learn to be content
happier than I
CENTENNIAL
200th ANNIVERSARY - THE BIRTH OF BETSY ROSS
3c
5c
PLANT for a more BEAUTIFUL AMERICA
CENTENNIAL OF SOUND RECORDING

INTRODUCTION

VICTORIA EDITOR-IN-CHIEF PHYLLIS HOFFMAN DEPIANO was dedicated to traditions of correspondence. While learning cursive in her girlhood days, she became enamored with fine stationery and fountain pens. In fact, when she was in the fifth grade, a friend's peacock blue ink so captivated Phyllis that many years later, she was delighted to find a glass bottle of the brilliant hue. The unopened vial remained a prized possession, reminding her of the incomparable beauty of handwritten reflections.

Phyllis also appreciated creative pursuits, such as calligraphy and letterpress, and championed those who turn these endeavors into businesses of bliss. She not only supported vendors with her patronage but also in the pages of the magazine.

However, even more than she adored accoutrements and artistry, she valued the deep and abiding connections formed through the exchange of missives. She once challenged readers to commit to writing to a different person at least once a week, noting that such a practice would change the lives of both sender and recipient. "It removes us from the whirl around us and takes us to thoughts of admiration, love, encouragement, and prayers," she said, adding, "It will make your heart happy and theirs." May this volume serve as a love letter to her legacy.

THE HERMITAGE
U.S. POSTAGE
Architecture USA 15c
Merci Merci
Dear Elizabeth,
Thank you for your gracious hospitality over the holidays. It was a pleasure getting to spend time with you and your beautiful family. I look forward to our next visit.
Fondly,
Catherine
Merci Merci

Like satin streamers unfurled back and forth across the miles, missives exchanged over the course of time tug gently at the heartstrings, pulling loved ones closer as each handwritten note further entwines the lives of sender and receiver.

A Life IN LETTERS

TEXT MELISSA LESTER

Several years ago, my grandmother surprised our family by returning all the letters we had written to her over the years. I was astonished to learn that, for more than forty years, she saved every piece of personal correspondence in its original stamped envelope.

My mother was the most faithful pen pal, usually writing at least once a week. Her letters chronicled our family's life, from her courtship with my father, through their early days of marriage, to the years of child raising, and beyond. What an unexpected gift it has been to glimpse snapshots of years past, reliving many long-forgotten events through witty observations and newsy tidbits.

Charity Girl

Although fewer in number, my own letters take me back to my youth. From preschool drawings of rainbows to the notes penned when my children were babies, I have enjoyed the nostalgia that rereading this correspondence has brought. Even seeing old stationery and address labels opens a floodgate of memories.

I remember sitting at the kitchen table as a kindergartner, laboriously printing thank-you notes on now yellowed, lined paper with cartoon animals in the corner. I giggle and roll my eyes at my fat, loopy adolescent handwriting—*Is* dotted with hearts, of course—penned on notebook paper folded like origami. Then, in my more familiar grown-up script, I reread floral postcards jotted hastily from my college dorm room, embossed ivory monogrammed note cards penned in my apartment as a newlywed, and teacup-themed stationery written in a quiet spot in our home while little ones slept nearby.

Bundled together, all these letters tell the tale of my journey to womanhood. I'm so grateful that my grandmother felt that this was a story worth preserving.

Receiving this treasury of letters has reminded me how precious personal correspondence can be. "We lay aside letters never to read them again, and at last we destroy them out of discretion," Johann Wolfgang von Goethe lamented, "and so disappears the most beautiful, the most immediate breath of life, irrecoverable for ourselves and for others."

I am now determined to keep my children's letters so that, years from now, each one can read through his or her life in letters, knowing that each word, memory, and sentiment shared was savored and cherished by a mother who was sincerely theirs.

SEALED WITH *Symbolism*

Like pausing for a cup of tea, letter writing is a lesson in beauty and grace. Elevating these small moments of contemplation, perhaps by finishing the envelopes with an ornate wax emblem, makes them even more special.

The Lake Isle of Innisfree
by William Butler Yeats
I will arise and go now, and go to Innisfree,
And a small cabin build there of clay and wattles made,
Nine bean rows will I have there, a hive for the honey bee,
And live alone in the bee-loud glade.
And I shall have some peace there, for peace comes dropping slow,
Dropping from the veils of the morning to where the cricket sings;
There midnight's all a glimmer, and noon a purple glow,
And evening full of the linnet's wings.
I will arise and go now, for always night and day
I hear lake water lapping with low sounds by the shore;
While I stand on the roadway, or on the pavements grey,
I hear it in the deep heart's core.

aanteekenen
R 's GRAVENHAGE
Willem de Zwijgerlaan
Gv. Wz.
Nº 169
U. S.
SEP
7
1945
NAVY
UNITED STATES POSTAGE
3 CENTS 3

Well-versed in the art of the wax seal, both its antique and modern uses, the artist behind Kathryn Hastings & Co. collects—and shares with the world—a breathtaking array of seals, custom waxes, and, perhaps most importantly, the stories behind them. While these signets were originally intended to secure a letter and prove the sender's identity, later eras saw them evolve to carry great symbolism. Black wax was used to share grave news, pink for congratulations—even the raised designs had meaning, giving a hint to the message that lay within.

GEORGE
ELIOT
GEORGE
ELIOT

Today, the metaphor behind some motifs may have shifted with culture, but each still carries a unique purpose. Whether the sender uses a custom seal for all letters—a crest signifying one's personality or family history—or uses various motifs to symbolize the words tucked inside, a wax seal certainly adds sentiment to one's correspondence and history to one's desk.

THE LOST ART OF HANDWRITTEN LETTERS

TEXT KATHLEEN THOMPSON

As you sort through the mail, the letter stands out. The envelope has a nice texture and a pleasing color. The stamp is floral, and the address is written in a beautiful hand. Turning the letter over, you notice it is sealed with pale blue wax and imprinted with a fleur-de-lis. A wedding invitation, no doubt, you think to yourself. Yet when you break the seal and slip out the contents, you discover a letter from an old friend. Delighted, you sit down in a chair and peruse the missive, smiling and perhaps rereading sections.

In this era of e-mails, texts, and cell phones, such an experience is rare but well worth reviving. My adventures in letter writing began with a complaint from my friend Ro. Since high school, we have maintained our friendship, despite living 700 miles apart. We wrote letters for many years, but with the advent of electronic communication, they became few and far between.

"I actually think I used to write more, before computers came on the scene," Ro lamented. "It is so much easier to write as I am doing now, sitting at a keyboard, watching the words appear on a screen. But I suspect something has been lost." I agreed, so my friend and I vowed to resume writing letters by hand.

Procuring the necessary supplies can be a challenge. I found that many card shops and bookstores offer only a limited selection. Not to be discouraged, we both scoured multiple locations and soon came up with several pretty papers. Seals and wax can be purchased in the wedding section at most stationery stores. It may seem like a contradiction, but letter-writing supplies can also be ordered online.

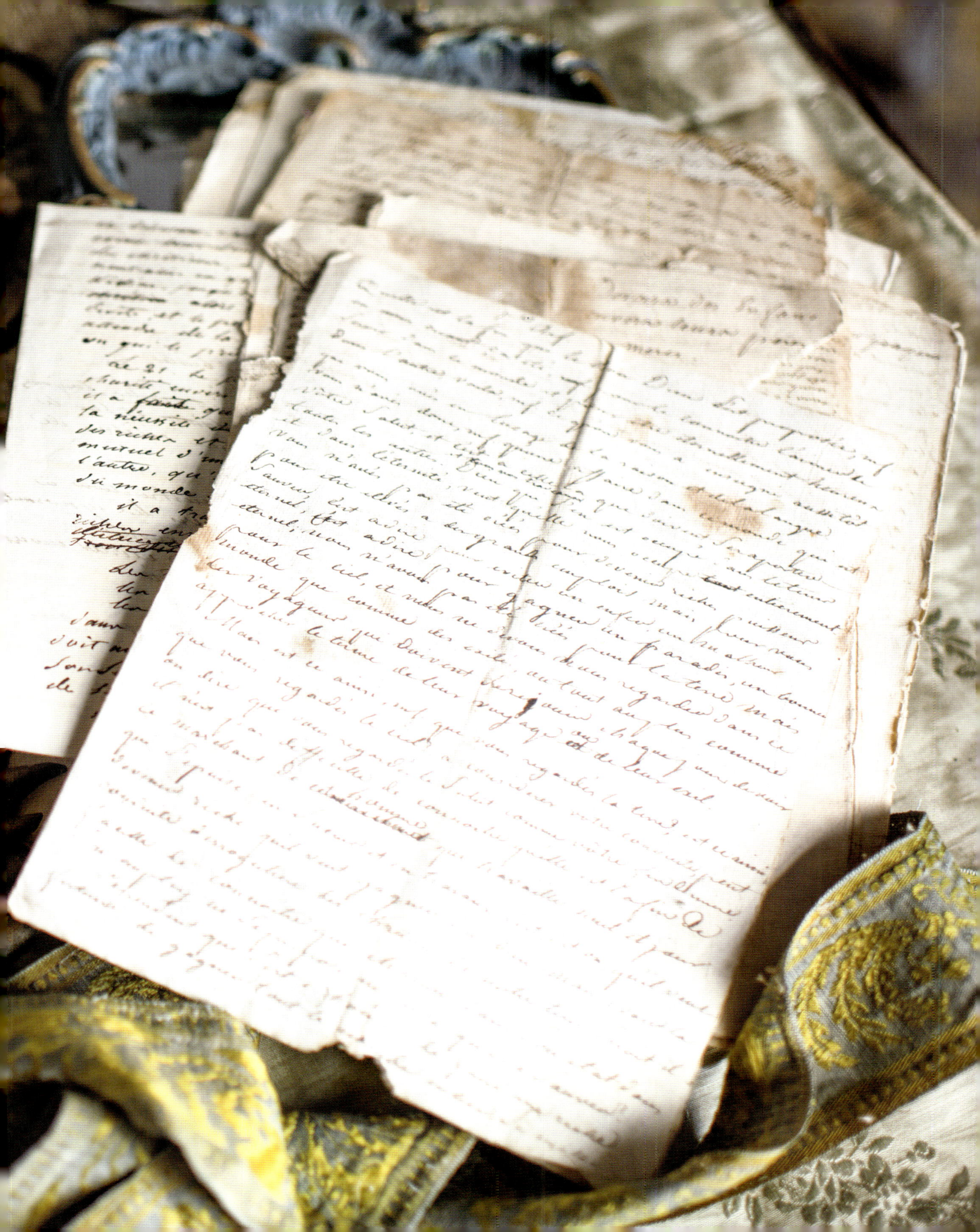

Choosing a pen is critical. I absolutely ruled out any type of ballpoint as too ordinary. In the beginning, I tried a crow quill dip pen and india ink. In my mind, I pictured myself as Abigail Adams writing to John or as a heroine in a Jane Austen novel. Alas, that was not to be. My penmanship was scratchy looking and the sound, annoying. Worse yet was the constant threat of a spill, resulting in a disaster of one kind or another.

Then I brought home a dozen pens of all kinds—from fine-point, permanent-ink varieties to newer styles. After much research, I recommend a blue or black gel pen. Today's fountain pens are also good choices, as the pop-in ink cartridges make them easier to handle.

Learning how to properly use sealing wax and a wax stamp was an exercise in hilarity. My first try set off the smoke alarm. The next was attempted beneath the overhead fan above my stove. This time I failed to notice the position of the design on the seal, which was an elegant *K* for my first name. I was proud I had achieved such a nice result, with no drips at the edges. Then I discovered that the initial was upside down!

Finding a relaxing time and place to write is the most enjoyable part of my new hobby. I prefer late in the evening, when the house is quiet and I am alone, my family having gone to bed. I find it is easier to share intimate feelings through this form of communication. Perhaps it is the fact that I set aside a tranquil period for writing versus my typical rush when dashing off e-mails on my computer.

Letter writing is best enjoyed with a close friend. Choose a correspondent (perhaps one who lives far away), and suggest making a writing pact. Ro and I still send e-mails, mostly regarding time-sensitive or mundane issues. On occasion we e-mail an alert that a letter has been posted, heightening our anticipation.

Now that I have acquired a collection of supplies, I have assembled a small kit housed in a lovely antique box. In another box, I keep Ro's letters, tied together with a soft ribbon, waiting to be relished and reread. Late at night, I set up my writing space, and there I reveal my deepest thoughts to a friend who has known and understood me most of my life. Through this shared pastime, our separation seems less so, and our connection has been strengthened, letter by letter.

Setting aside a physical space where the accoutrements of correspondence sit within easy reach not only helps organize the home but also encourages one to carve out time for establishing a regular practice of putting pen to paper.

PURSUIT OF *Loveliness*

Long before modern methods of communication were conceived, the practice of exchanging letters linked hearts and minds in a way spoken words could not—an indelible legacy that lingers still.

British poet Lord Byron is commonly credited with noting, "Letter writing is the only device for combining solitude with good company." How true is this observation! Alone at the desk, with a gentle fire kindling at the hearth, words pour out in flowery flourishes as if one's very soul is speaking with a dear friend so far away yet so near in thoughts.

Creating a serene spot for penning handwritten messages not only fosters lyrical prose, it also connects the correspondent to generations of women who have taken pen in hand to scribe the innermost breathings of the heart upon the page.

Opposite: An antique letter box beautifully corrals writing paraphernalia. Clockwise from above left: Offerings included in the subtly textured matte-finish Modern suite from The Wells Makery have the softly ruffled look of handmade paper. A small leather lockbox holds an assortment of vintage postage stamps from Prints Charming Soho; more of the company's vast inventory of history-brushed items mingles with antique brass desk accessories—nostalgic mementos from another time.

Opposite: Calligraphy by Annie Brooks—one half of the creative duo known as The Wells Makery—illustrates the timeless allure of this handwrought art. This page, above right and center left: Vintage postage stamps, antique papers, and wax seals from Prints Charming Soho echo the artistry of bygone days. Below right: The florid script of Jennifer Reynolds, whose work is also seen on pages 114 and 115, bestows gilded ornamentation to an invitation. Below left: Renaissance-style papers line envelopes handmade by Papira Designs & Letterpress.

A SPACE TO *Reflect*

The invitation to pause for a moment to pen a letter to a friend or to jot an entry into a diary is unspoken in this serene space but keenly felt. Setting aside a corner for personal correspondence enhances the enjoyment of a personal retreat.

In the charming Marais district of Paris, Hôtel Caron de Beaumarchais extends a warm welcome to guests. In this lovely petal-strewn sanctuary, a desk positioned to take in views of the City of Light encourages one to while away the hours, a cup of tea in hand, while reflecting on memories of the sights and sounds of a Gallic sojourn. The look of this luxurious auberge offers inspiration for cultivating similarly inviting environs at home.

Inkwells: AN INDELIBLE PART OF OUR PAST

With a pen dipped into an owl-shaped inkwell in 1875, Louisa May Alcott crafted sentences into art to create some of the most enduring pieces of American literature.

Inkwells like the one Alcott treasured were essential tools in the nineteenth century, when carefully written letters were often the only link to loved ones, and business deals were scripted and sealed with wax. The first inkwells were developed by the ancient Romans and used throughout the ages by other civilizations. But by the early 1900s, when the more practical fountain pen was developed, inkwells had largely been abandoned.

Admirers have resurrected these vintage desktop vessels, and the wells have become coveted collectibles. Inkwells come in hundreds of shapes and styles—from the "very plain and functional to the ornate and whimsical," says Barbara Bureker, a collector and merchant in Battle Ground, Washington. She especially favors those that show ink stains and other subtle signs of wear, as these make it easier for her to imagine the many decades of history the objects have witnessed.

Inkwells made from ornate, moulded glass or exquisitely painted porcelain are treasures and models of enduring elegance. Others, like a white milk-glass inkwell in the shape of a cottage or a wooden turtle concealing ink below its shell, are more fanciful. Collectors also seek umbrella-shaped glass inkwells, with a narrow, circular spout on top and a flared base. Teakettle- and domed-shaped inkwells with offset necks are also prized pieces.

Although some collectors specialize, hunting for inkwells made of a certain material or by a particular manufacturer, most are simply charmed by the unique shape and design of each specimen. Some are dazzling and others intriguing, but every inkwell captures the imagination.

Stationery SUITE

One of the joys of cultivating a practice of correspondence is collecting a range of beautiful papers. Choosing from the cache a note card perfectly suited to the recipient or occasion increases the pleasure of moments invested in writing letters to loved ones.

Miscellaneous
Pianoforte Works
LA RIGOLETTA
MAKE YOUR

Blooming with favorite varieties, from roses to hydrangeas, floral stationery remains perennially popular. Gilding adds a special touch to the suite below, while watercolor designs shown opposite draw the eye with depictions of bouquets, a topiary, and blue-and-white porcelain.

TREASURE CHEST

When a bedroom or living area does not allow for a full-size desk or a dedicated area for correspondence, an array of collectibles can add beauty to interiors while keeping necessary accoutrements within easy reach. Clockwise from above left: Tea caddies can house stamps, stationery, and other sundries. Lap desks, also known as writing cabinets, rose to popularity in the eighteenth and nineteenth centuries for their convenience and portability. Often fashioned from hardwoods and embellished with intricate details, these antique finds can turn a bed or small table into a peaceful nook for recording reflections.

Noble IMPRESSIONS

While living in England, former Artist-in-Residence Stephanie Monahan became captivated with heraldic emblems and the implements that pressed their intricate designs into small puddles of melted wax. Personalized insignias were used centuries ago to establish a document's official nature, verify the sender's identity, and ensure private correspondence.

Stephanie's foray into collecting these relics began with livery buttons—trimmings that distinguished the uniforms of all male servants in a particular household—but soon developed into a quest for pieces more rare. Among her most valuable finds are an Italian signet ring bearing a stately cameo and two French stamps that once belonged to royalty. Within the yellowed pages of an antique book, she discovered a cache of wax seals from as far back as the 1700s, preserved long ago by some kindred spirit.

The artisan frames original seals in shadow boxes and uses the stamps to create her own hallmarks, thereby showcasing the enduring beauty of unique heirlooms and offering a tactile connection to the past.

Les Années 1790 et 1791
Conséquence de la fuite
la situation semble précaire

A *Desk* OF HER OWN

When the lady of the house can claim a spot for contemplation, she has room to wander halls of memory and ponder realms of possibility. Amid the bustling seas of modern family life, bouquets of freshly cut blossoms and a careful selection of keepsakes make the vignette a treasured isle of tranquility.

At Hills & Dales, a historic estate in LaGrange, Georgia, the wedding dress of former matriarch Alice Hand Callaway graces a chair. Personal effects on the desk include a portrait of her mother, Florence Hand, and a unique turtle clock. Come evening, the lamp yields a gentle glow.

LOVELY PENS

The quest for a single magnificent writing instrument can evolve quickly into a collection of varied yet impressive implements. Aficionados often prefer a certain type of material for the barrel, from an engraved platinum-plated metal that boasts the look of sterling silver to a sleek celluloid or polished wood. A favored pen feels comfortable and well-balanced in the hand. When considering a fountain pen, the uninked nib should glide easily over a sheet of paper. For other styles, such as ballpoint or roller ball, the mechanism for extending and retracting the writing tip should be as smooth as the flow of ink across a piece of fine stationery.

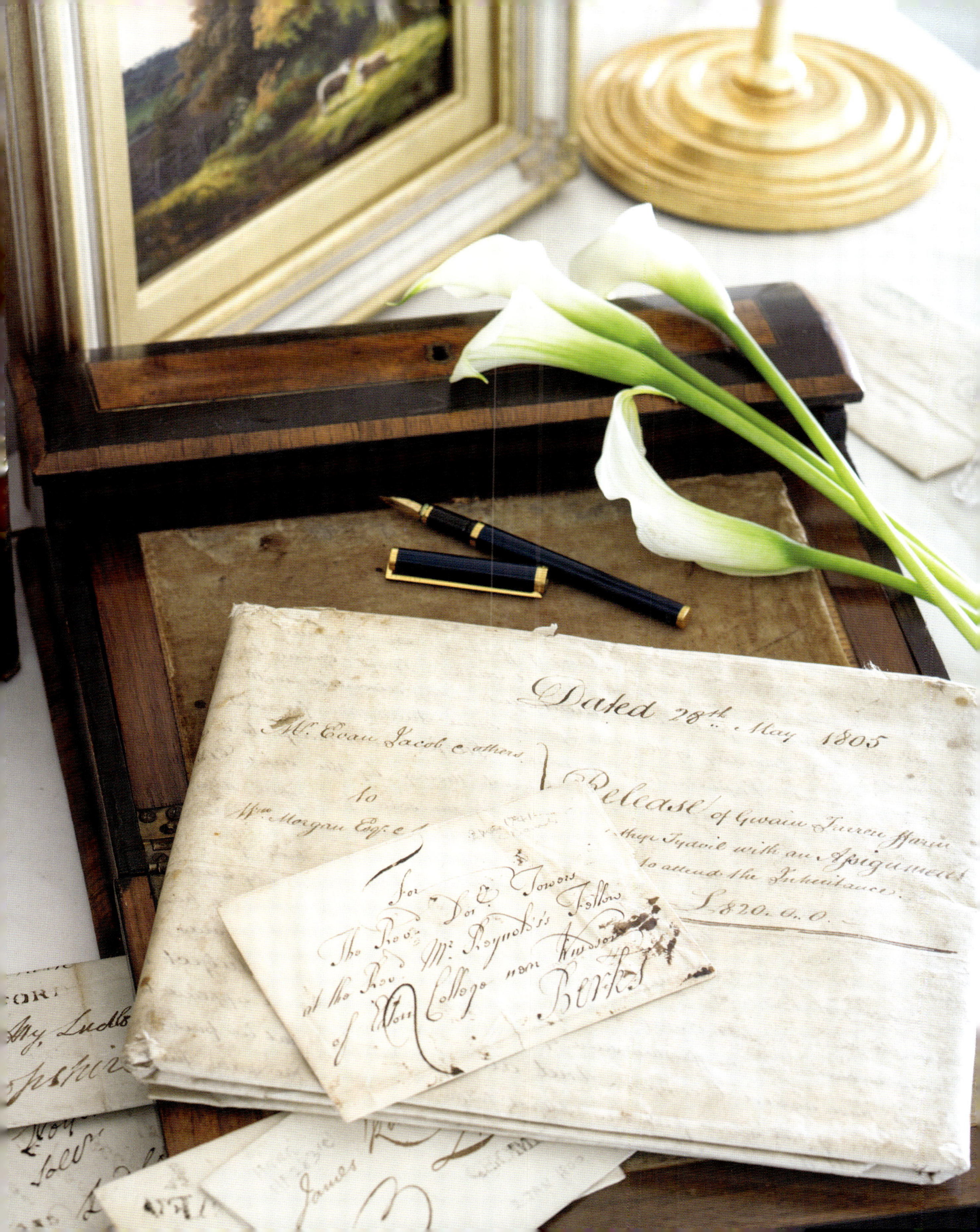
Dated 28th May 1805
Release
£820. 0. 0.
Berks

Miss Sally Jones
32 Primrose Lane
Mobile, AL
36123

PRESTIGIOUS ADDRESS

The thoughtfulness expressed in a missive can continue to the envelope that will convey those sentiments to the intended recipient. Seeing one's own handwritten address in a familiar script prompts the immediate, joyful recognition of greetings from a faithful pen pal, while viewing the same information in an elegantly calligraphed font sets the tone for a special announcement or invitation. The method used for adding the return address adds to the initial impression, and even the choice of postage stamp can serve to further reflect the occasion, season, or holiday.

20th May 1717
Enfranchisement
of a Close called Holme
Richd Beeby
NORGE 20
Official First Day Cover
SAINT LOUIS, MO.
MAR 17
7:30 PM
1958
GARDENING HORTICULTURE
U.S. POSTAGE 3¢
POSTAL CARD - ONE CENT.
United States of America
THIS SIDE IS FOR THE ADDRESS ONLY.
BATH
QUEENS, N.Y.
C. H. Ward Esq
Cottage Gardens
Queens Long Island
N.Y.
Dated 24th December 1805
COTE FRANCAISE DES SOMALIS
THOMAS JEFFERSON
UNITED STATES
DELIVERY
TEN CENTS
U.S. POSTAGE
PROVIDENCE
HILTONS
APR 14
1898
VA.
POSTAL CARD - ONE CENT.
United States of America
THIS SIDE IS FOR THE ADDRESS ONLY.

PRESERVING PIECES OF POSTAL HISTORY

The culture of mail and postage carries a universal mystique—where a letter or postcard originated, where it traveled, and where it ultimately came to rest.

The notion that technology has trumped written correspondence, and has diminished stamp collecting, is little more than that: a notion. Vicky Fenimore, a stamp collector for more than fifty years, is witness to a resurgence in the hobby, as adults are revisiting their collections and inviting their children and grandchildren to join in.

A member of one of the most established stamp-collecting clubs in the country, the Lynchburg (Virginia) Stamp Club (formed in 1932), Vicky has visited elementary schools and taught beginner classes to ensure that the hobby passes to the next generation. Eager to share their love of animals or sports, the children are surprised and delighted when she reaches into her large box and retrieves stamps with these images. Thus, a new fascination with stamps is born.

In the United States alone, 25 million people are devoted stamp collectors, also known as philatelists. Worldwide, that figure jumps to 200 million. With more than a half-million stamp issues in circulation between 1840 and today, a collector can gather stamps based on a theme or topic, categorize pieces into a more manageable collection, and continue for years.

Stamp collecting has enjoyed such longevity because of the increase in issues from countries around the globe, a greater diversity in subjects, and the presence of the Internet, which allows for easier buying and selling.

In previous generations, the subjects of postage stamps were limited to "kings, queens, and dead men," says Ken Martin, director of expertizing of the American Philatelic Society. In the 1950s and '60s, the release of topical or thematic stamps launched a new wave of collecting, with U.S. stamps featuring holidays, classic cars, and landmarks. In the 1970s and '80s, the hobby grew to include postal history, when collectors began to seek stamps still affixed to postcards and envelopes (preferably with the original letters tucked inside).

Vicky, on the other hand, collects postcards for their postmarks and canceled stamps. "I couldn't care less about the pictures." She laughs. Her preference for postmarks illustrates her own theory that stamp collecting has no rules. She explains, "You can collect stamps any way you want to."

Although postage has experienced changes, stamp collecting remains largely the same as it was for previous enthusiasts. "The hobby can be enjoyed by all ages," Ken says. "The older you are, the more that nostalgia plays into it."

If you haven't collected in years, he adds, you can easily return. The trend among philatelists historically has been to stray during their teenage and young-adult years, then to resume the hobby in their 30s and 40s. That's the beauty of such a timeless pursuit, says Ken. "You can always come back to it."

Letter OPENERS

Antiques dealers may debate whether the terms "paper knife" and "letter opener" can be used interchangeably—with some pointing to the paper knife's origins centuries ago as a tool to slit the uncut edges of books—but collectors are certain to find common ground on the value and beauty of these essential desk accessories.

Shanghai
Monsieur
l'abbé Boutaud

Considering their practicality for everyday use, the letter opener makes an ideal gift for a friend or colleague, with the range of styles available nearly infinite. Handles of sterling silver, crystal, and porcelain bring to mind the appeal of favorite patterns associated with tableware, while those of bamboo or brass offer nods to a more classic executive look. The artfulness of many antique designs—especially those hand-carved in ivory or fashioned from mother-of-pearl—is truly remarkable. Chosen to suit the tastes of the recipient, such an implement is likely to be enjoyed daily as both an objet d'art and an oft-used utensil.

CALL TO SERVICE

Calling cards, once a gatekeeper to social interactions, have been employed around the world for centuries. Some historians believe they appeared as early as the 1500s in China. Their popularity blossomed in eighteenth-century Europe and reached a golden age in America during the late nineteenth century, when intricate rules of etiquette were at play. For instance, a first-time gentleman visitor would place his card on the butler's silver server and leave. The vessel, also known as "a waiter," would be presented to the lady of the house, and if she returned her card, the meeting was arranged. If nothing was sent back, it was an indication she didn't desire to pursue the friendship. Other customs, such as folding certain corners of the card, communicated an assortment of meanings from congratulations to condolences.

Such intrigue transpired through the use of calling card trays. As recently as the 1970s, a silver tray would be set near the entrance at coffees and teas, large gatherings that were popular among women at the time. Attendees would drop their social cards in the tray to be certain the hostess knew they had stopped by. While that practice has fallen by the wayside, the vintage salvers remain for the clever hostess to concoct new uses, both for parties and everyday affairs.

Add a little glamour to your appetizer buffet by loading several of the small platters with bites of savory fare, or use them to elevate tiny bonbons and cookies at the end of a meal. Just before guests arrive for an evening of entertainment, a tray layered with fresh aromatic herbs makes for a welcoming scent in an entryway. Perfect as a coaster, no shine required, they are bound to spark conversation. A sugar bowl and creamer fit perfectly in the limited space.

The pretty pieces also elevate home décor, arranged in groupings on a shelf or on a wall. They can add elegance to a powder room as a soap dish (with a glass liner for protection) or as a hand-towel holder. On your desk, position a notepad in one or place daily mail awaiting review.

Ideas are endless, so you can easily devise your own schemes for these lovelies that recall centuries of intrigue and delight in personal communications. Or with the upswing in personal cards as part of a stationery suite, set one out at your next event and see if you garner a few.

ADVENTURES OF HAJJI BABA
VOL. II
VOL. III

words,
And
you close."

Legendary LETTERS

Many of the most celebrated authors in all of literature have also been prolific in terms of their personal communications, leaving behind treasuries of private reflections that offer glimpses of their innermost hopes and longings.

JANE AUSTEN

With her quill pen poised above simple yet elegant cream-colored stationery, beloved British novelist Jane Austen allowed her musings about life in late eighteenth-century England to flow as freely as if she were conversing in person. Though she penned thousands of letters in her lifetime, correspondence with her sister, Cassandra, exemplified Jane's keen powers of observation, joyful outlook, and clever wit. Every social event was described in minute detail, drawing Cassandra into the scene as if she herself were present.

Wednesday 15 - Friday 17 June

My dearest Cassandra

Where shall I begin? Which of my important nothings shall I tell you first? At half after seven yesterday morning Henry saw us into our carriage, and we drove away from Bath Hotel; which, by the bye, had been found most uncomfortable quarters— very dirty, very noisy and very ill provided. James began his journey by coach at five. Our first eight miles were hot; Deptford Hill brought to my mind our hot journey into Kent fourteen years ago

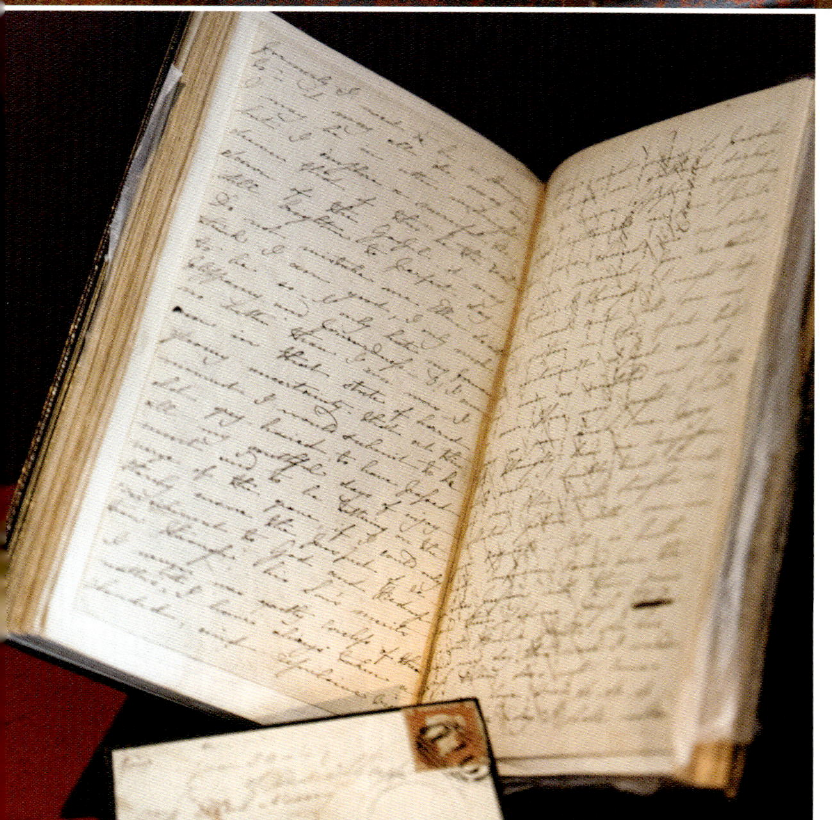

THE BRONTË SISTERS

While residing with their widowed father in Haworth Parsonage, this trio of stair-step siblings shared an affinity for writing, whether it was the novels that brought them recognition in the literary world or personal correspondence penned to friends. Charlotte was the most prolific, and her missives offered an intimate narrative of the three sisters' lives. Along with Emily and Anne, she often wrote "cross" letters, as was the style of the day, with sentences written both horizontally and vertically to save on the costly per-page price of postage.

LORD BYRON

As one of the prominent poets of England's Romantic movement, Lord Byron created a considerable cache of rhapsodic verse that enthralled eighteenth-century audiences. His missives reflect this same lyrical style, though often peppered with witty commentary and tales from his travels. Whether written from his venerable desk at Newstead Abbey—his home in Nottinghamshire—or from a balcony with a view to the Mediterranean Sea, Lord Byron's myriad letters reveal a short but colorful life.

OXFORD UNIVERSITY CALENDAR 1952
THREE NUNS
RATION BOOK
KELLY'S DIRECTORY OF OXFORDSHIRE
JOHNSON'S OXFORD FOR TIMBER

C. S. LEWIS

The thought-provoking works of author and literary scholar C. S. Lewis reflect his spiritual conversion from nonbeliever to ardent theologian. Best known for his Narnia series, Lewis composed his prose at a desk overlooking the back garden of The Kilns, his home in Oxford, England. His often poignant letters, penned to companions, colleagues, and curious readers, evince a man willing to encourage others. In a note to his friend J. R. R. Tolkien upon reading *The Lord of the Rings*, he said, "I have drained the rich cup and satisfied a long thirst."

JOHN KEATS

While many of his fellow Romantic poets penned essays extolling the praises of poetry, John Keats preferred to plead his case in correspondence with family and friends, where his beautiful words portrayed verse as a form of art. His letters are written in a rather breathless, stream-of-consciousness fashion, strung together with a series of dashes, and often included lines of poetry, as well. Keats was quick to praise his contemporaries but saved his highest accolades for his most admired bard, William Shakespeare.

BEATRIX POTTER

In breathing life into a menagerie of whimsical characters inspired by the resident critters of her Hill Top Farm, British watercolorist and author Beatrix Potter created a magical world that has charmed generations of children and adults. In "picture letters" to family and friends, Beatrix delighted recipients with tiny sketches of winsome animals accompanying her words. In fact, *The Tale of Peter Rabbit* traces its beginnings to a missive sent to the five-year-old son of her former governess.

"LIFE IS A LUMINOUS HALO, A SEMI-TRANSPARENT ENVELOPE SURROUNDING US FROM THE BEGINNING OF CONSCIOUSNESS TO THE END."

—Virginia Woolf

VIRGINIA WOOLF

As a member of an illustrious coterie of creatives and critical thinkers—known as the Bloomsbury group for the London neighborhood where they gathered—author Virginia Woolf discovered kinship and support for her writing endeavors within this distinguished circle. She found solace in correspondence, once penning, "Life would split asunder without letters." Virginia often exchanged epistles with her sister Vanessa, a painter and designer who was also among the Bloomsbury set, wistfully recalling their childhood visits to the scenic Cornwall coast.

A Room of One's Own
Virginia Woolf
VIRGINIA WOOLF
The Common Reader Vol.I
MRS DALLOWAY

OURNALS
OF
OROTHY
VOL. II
Edited by

WILLIAM WORDSWORTH

Though his works covered a variety of themes, English Romantic poet William Wordsworth penned ballads that often illustrated his belief that an appreciation for nature was essential to one's soul. His family home in the picturesque Lake District not only offered ample inspiration for some of his most notable poems but was also the hearth of a happy life with his wife, Mary. Whenever business called him away, the couple exchanged sweet letters, exchanging newsy tidbits—and reaffirming their ardent love and devotion.

Sorry
to hear you're
not
feeling well...

Sentiments SHARED

Bearing in mind the proverb that asserts that a fitting word is like "apples of gold in settings of silver," we offer guidance for penning thoughtful greetings, whether the intention is to deliver a message of appreciation, comfort, or congratulations.

harlotte Collier
El Bosque
anta Barbara, CA
93108
THANK YOU
thank you

IN GRATITUDE

Penning a thank-you note allows one to reflect not only on a single act but also on the greater impact that the giver has had on the life of the receiver. Expressing gratitude for a kindness may be the impetus for writing—and a prompt and sincere acknowledgment is certain to be appreciated—but going beyond the requisite affirmations of the good deed and its benefits will make the letter all the more meaningful. Take a few moments to put into words the lasting effects of the individual's presence, example, or encouragement, and the missive becomes a treasure to keep forever.

THINKING OF YOU

A walk to the mailbox becomes a lovely highlight of the afternoon when a pretty, personalized envelope awaits among the more mundane offerings. Despite the recognition that such a surprise is sure to provoke delight, without a special circumstance or occasion spurring the effort, plans to jot a few lines to a friend can be lost to the busyness of the day. A few ideas for establishing the practice of sending greetings are to devote a window of time to the task each week, to make a list of people to whom you wish to write, and to post each letter without delay.

A POSY FOR YOU
My Sweet Friend
Pink Rose; grace, joy
Sweet Pea; delicate pleasures
Delphinium; well-being
Stock; lasting beauty
Wooly Bush; gentleness
Fern; sincerity
Tweedia; hearts that believe in each other

If you're alone, I'll
be your shadow.
If you want to cry,
I'll be your shoulder.
If you want a hug,
I'll be your pillow.
If you want to be happy,
I'll be your smile.
But anytime you need
a friend. I'll just be me.

WITH SYMPATHY

When someone suffers a great loss, an outpouring of thoughtful gestures serves as a balm for the spirit. Among the most comforting keepsakes are handwritten condolences, from a simple promise of prayer to a heartfelt recounting of special memories. Especially uplifting to one who is grieving are remembrances that reflect the deceased's care—"Your mother's eyes always sparkled when she spoke about you"—or shed light on a new story—"Let me tell you about the summer that your grandfather and I set out on an adventure." Bearing in mind that holidays and anniversaries can bring new waves of grief, sending cards throughout the year can be a way to lend support as the months pass. Offers to help are best followed with a phone call to suggest and solidify plans.

CORDIALLY INVITED

From an intimate tea party to the most grand and elaborate wedding, an exquisite invitation sets the scene for an unforgettable gathering. The text opens with a welcoming phrase, such as "We request the honor of your presence," and continues with all the information needed for attending the event. Along with this verbiage, the look of the piece offers clues to the aesthetics and level of formality that guests can expect. Grace notes, such as wax seals or satin bows, further enhance the beauty of the overture.

OAKWOOD AVENUE
SAVANNAH, GEORGIA
KINDLY REPLY
BY THE TWENTIETH OF MARCH
M
ACCEPT(S) WITH PLEASURE
DECLINE(S) WITH REGRET
MR. AND MRS. JACOB BENNETT SCOTT
REQUEST THE PLEASURE OF YOUR COMPANY
AT THE MARRIAGE OF THEIR DAUGHTER
ANNE CHARLOTTE
TO
MICAH JAMES ADAMS
SATURDAY, THE TWENTY-SECOND OF MAY
TWO THOUSAND AND TWENTY-SEVEN
AT SIX O'CLOCK IN THE EVENING
THE MACKEY HOUSE
SAVANNAH, GEORGIA
DINNER AND DANCING TO FOLLOW
TOGETHER WITH THEIR FAMILIES
Emma Elizabeth
AND
Jonathan Dean Pittman
REQUEST THE PLEASURE OF YOUR COMPANY
AT THEIR WEDDING
SATURDAY, THE NINETEENTH OF DECEMBER
TWO THOUSAND TWENTY
AT FIVE O'CLOCK IN THE EVENING
The Barn at Collins Family Farm
COBBTOWN, GEORGIA
TO FOLLOW

Sending Love

GET WELL SOON

Facing injury or illness can be wearying to both body and spirit, and a card can provide a needed boost to someone who is feeling under the weather. Well wishes should offer care, empathy, and support. When accompanying the message with a meal, be mindful of what foods would be easiest to eat or most appropriate to the patient's situation, and inquire, when possible, about a family's dietary restrictions or preferences beforehand. Including a book or magazine, a bouquet of fresh-cut flowers that do not have a strong fragrance, or another small token can cast a bit of sunshine into what could be a long and dreary time of recovery. For the one who is healing, the greatest relief comes in knowing that he or she is not alone in the journey toward better health.

"MERRIMENT COMES IN SPARKS, JOY IN FLASHES, AND HAPPINESS IN LIGHTNINGS."

—Stanley Haskins

GLAD TIDINGS

Happiness is amplified when it is shared, and this adage applies especially to life's most precious milestones. Such significant transitions as graduating, accepting a marriage proposal, embarking on a new job or career, or welcoming a baby are enjoyed to the fullest when celebrated in community. Sending announcements serves to mark these special moments; receiving such a greeting invites one into the circle of joy. When good news comes, respond with a gift or a sincere note declaring your hearty felicitations.

5410 GREYSTONE WAY
E
WE WELCOME WITH LOVE
Emma Jane Darden
JANUARY 17, 2014
7 POUNDS, 4 OUNCES
19 1/2 INCHES
KELLY, DUSTY & AVERY
Every good and perfect gift is from above
James 1:17

10th Anniversary
10

CONGRATULATIONS
Commemorate an acquaintance or colleague's achievements with positive words that honor what you have observed of the person's character and accomplishments. Celebrate a friend's victories with admiration for past dedication and hopeful expectation for future opportunities. Champion the successes of loved ones with encouraging messages that help them see their great value and sparking potential. Taking the time to notice, appreciate, and affirm the strengths of others creates an atmosphere of encouragement and support.

In every letter,
in every line,
she saw him.
Diana Peterfreund

Artful EXPRESSIONS

Where language falls short in conveying the fullness of affections, gifts of creativity can speak volumes, with the swirls of a hand-lettered script or the exquisite adornments on a custom note card revealing the musings of the heart.

WITH A *Delicate Hand*

Each movement of the nib, from the lightest hairline stroke to the most elaborate loop, creates lettering that is completely unique. Incorporating the gentle art of calligraphy into correspondence makes every salutation extraordinary.

RS. WILLIAM
E HONOUR OF
RRIAGE OF T
with Seared
tails, Dinner an
AFTER FIVE O'C
SCOTTISH R

Bon Appetit
Plantillo
Oakville
1994
ROBERT MONDAVI
OAKVILLE DISTRICT
NAPA VALLEY
CABERNET SAUVIG
UNFILTERED
ALCOHOL 13.5% BY VOLUME
Hula
Wonderful Clothing and Gifts
36 La Salle Avenue Montclair, CA 94611 (510) 339-9385
return
to
estate
of
grace
Maison d'Etre

A special project to pursue is developing a bespoke monogram that can be incorporated into a personal or wedding suite of stationery. When conceived for an individual, the cipher becomes a reflection of the client's inimitable style. In sketching designs for an engaged couple, calligrapher Allison R. Banks seeks to represent both personalities. When blending disparate tastes of bride and groom, she suggests meeting in the middle with a classic initial for their surname, a feminine initial for her, and a masculine initial for him. The layering and intertwining of letterforms creates an enchanting symbol of marital bliss.

Hilary
Dave Pellicciaro &
Stephanie Loucas
1097 57th Street, Unit B
Emeryville, California 94608
Mr. & Mrs.
Aaron Rubenstein
TABLE 6
Mr. & Mrs.
Esteban Barbano
TABLE 2
Jennifer
Biederback
Ms. Emma
Rousseau
With joyful hearts
SALLY AND GREG HARTMAN AND
DONNA AND ALLEN DORNAK
REQUEST THE PLEASURE OF YOUR COMPANY
AT THE MARRIAGE OF
Jessica Alice
and
Matthew Allen
SATURDAY
OCTOBER 25, 2014
FIVE O'CLOCK IN THE AFTERNOON
BURLINGAME COUNTRY CLUB
HILLSBOROUGH, CALIFORNIA
Dinner and dancing to follow
Coat and tie
Julie Berglund
Samantha Ahern
1270 Charles Street
Augusta, Georgia
30907

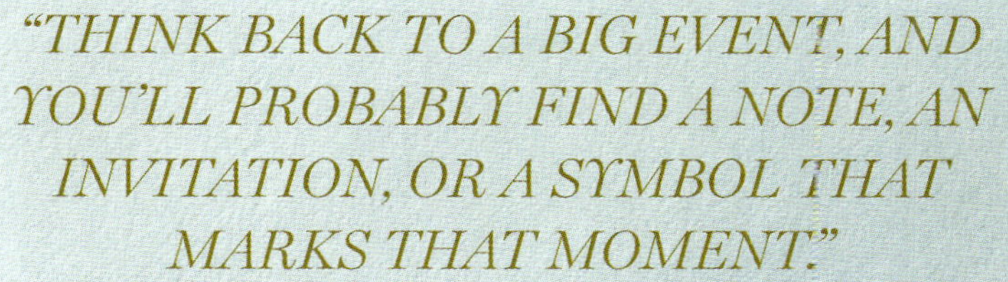

"THINK BACK TO A BIG EVENT, AND YOU'LL PROBABLY FIND A NOTE, AN INVITATION, OR A SYMBOL THAT MARKS THAT MOMENT."

—Allison R. Banks

Prints CHARMING

To create a mark of dignity, the traditional appeal of letterpress stationery endures as a timeless and elegant choice.

Invented by Johannes Gutenberg in the fifteenth century, the letterpress revolutionized the publishing industry, which had previously relied on more tedious block printing. Gutenberg's clever process involves reproducing designs through the repeated direct impression of an inked surface against the paper, resulting in letterforms and images with a raised finish. Although more modern methods of printing emerged from the eighteenth to twentieth centuries, the allure of a textured look remains strong. For correspondence that warrants a classic approach—from personal calling cards and holiday greetings to wedding invitations or business materials—letterpress offers a stylish option for customization. Select printshops maintain this possibility through masterful press operators who keep the artistic trade alive in the twenty-first century. For a similar effect, embossing creates a raised pattern in the paper itself through pressing the sheet between a pair of dies.

Sally
Karl
THE
MILL ROSE
INN
Moon Bay, CA 94019
96. 8750

Noteworthy IMPRESSIONS

Crafted individually by a highly skilled team, greeting and enclosure cards from Paula Skene Designs speak to the heart with vibrant, dimensional images. An unwavering commitment to excellence renders each one a collector's piece worthy of framing.

Thanks a Bunch

Thank You

Since Paula Skene Designs launched more than four decades ago, achievements have included developing merchandise for museums, corporate clients, and even a presidential inauguration luncheon. But perhaps dearer than these doors of opportunity are the windows her cards have opened—glimpses into the time lines of customers who mark important milestones with acknowledgments specially chosen for the occasion. "Sending a handwritten note is a bit like gathering around the table with good friends," says artist and entrepreneur Paula. "It's a way to connect. Considering all the issues we are facing globally, it means so much to receive something a little softer, a little more personal. It's a lift in the form of a card." To fashion her motifs, foil is applied to each illustration, a single color at a time, before the paper is embossed in a hand-carved brass die. All steps of production must be executed meticulously to create one unforgettable greeting card.

Leaf AND Petal

A sweet posy of flowers, tucked into a heavy book for safekeeping or dried using more contemporary methods, can become a precious bouquet for a pen pal when the dainty stems are affixed to a handmade card.

When choosing varieties to press, keep in mind that blossoms with a single row of petals will yield better results than those with bulkier heads. Forget-me-nots—a delightful selection for their symbolism and simple form—are an ideal pick. Other suitable stems are pansies, poppies, and perennial geraniums. The easiest technique is to arrange fresh-cut blooms inside a folded sheet of parchment paper, tuck the parchment into a heavy volume, place a weight on top of the book, and set aside for two to four weeks. Use tweezers to lift the dainty petals, brush the backs with clear glue, and secure to stationery.

Etched in MEMORY

Celebrating the best things in life, these personalized mementos honor precious moments of the past, present, and future.

Though photographs and journal entries keep record of memories we hold most dear, perhaps an even more extraordinary way to mark an experience is with a bespoke keepsake designed to be cherished. For centuries, artisans have chiseled intricate swirling scripts and ornate patterns into objets d'art to commemorate special occasions. An ancient skill, etching can be found in seashells and other natural elements dating back millennia. At the turn of the sixteenth century, a small unassuming hand tool known as the burin revolutionized artistic engraving and allowed craftsmen the ability to add dramatic flair and Baroque embellishments to metals and wood. In modern times, this delicate handiwork is still widely appreciated for its elegant appearance and heartfelt significance. Jennifer Reynolds Calligraphy's handcrafted etchings personalize even the tiniest treasures. The artisan uses a small engraving pen to perfect each coil of script and delicate design. A metallic wax-based putty enhances the inscriptions.

N°5
CHANEL
PARIS
EAU DE PARFUM

Two Hearts, One Dream
one I love
Valentine
To my Valentine
love

Season's GREETINGS

Although the close of the year prompts many well-wishers to reach out to kith and kin with a holiday card, the calendar provides opportunities throughout the year for spreading cheer through winter, spring, summer, and fall.

WILLIAM SHAKESPEARE
THOUGHTS
This above all:
to thine own self be true.
HAMLET

NEW YEAR'S WISHES

Opening a new calendar offers an ideal opportunity to reach out to loved ones far and wide with a hopeful message for the New Year, and this happy greeting can prompt a revived commitment to staying in touch as the months pass. When January begins with a faithful exchange of missives, the walk to the mailbox will grow more precious by the day from February to December.

BE MY VALENTINE

The sweetest sentiments, from quiet admiration to ardent affection, are aptly shared in midwinter when thoughts of friendship or flirtation warm even the frostiest of conditions. The celebration of Valentine's Day, a holiday originating in the fourteenth century, grew over time to include cards depicting symbols of devotion, such as Cupid, the Roman god of love. Hearts, flowers, and birds also figure prominently in these designs, with gifts of candy, fresh blooms, or jewelry traditional tokens. For collectors, vintage valentines offer intriguing connections to stories of romance written long ago.

To greet my love.

With true affection

"BUT IT WAS YOUR LETTER
WITHIN, DEAR HEART, MY FIRST
LOVE LETTER, AND SWEETER
TO ME THAN THE SUBTLEST
LOVE-LYRIC SAPPHO EVER
PENNED IN AEOLIC GOLD."
—Byron Caldwell Smith

Barbara
Menu
APPETIZER
MAIN DISH
chicken cordon bleu
DESSERT
tarte tatin

BRING MAY FLOWERS

Blossoming along with the spring verdure are the many holidays and special occasions that highlight this season. Following the observance of Easter comes the opportunity for celebrating May Day, with Mother's Day not long behind. A flurry of graduation announcements, bridal and baby shower invitations, and save-the-date cards for upcoming weddings also fill the mailbox with joy. A key for keeping up with all these delightful opportunities for correspondence is to plan ahead by gathering stationery and stamps and making note of any significant dates for RSVPs.

"THE CALL OF SPRING SEEMS TO BE LOUDER, SWEETER, MORE SIREN-LIKE, THAN EVER BEFORE."

—M. F. Canfield

Opposite: A tray brimming with floral note cards and a favorite pen allows one to pause for a few moments to pen a letter wherever and whenever inspiration strikes. On a windy day, one might prefer to write indoors, within view of an open window so that the billow of curtains frames the view of swaying branches. This page, below left: As the sun coaxes the landscape to awaken from its wintry rest, a comfortable spot in the garden offers a natural writing prompt. Simply chronicle the beauty of the scene, and enclose a few seeds or pressed petals as a tribute to the wonders you behold.

PENNING PATRIOTISM

Amid the merriment of national holidays, consider setting aside time to write to loved ones in the military—or to their families—to thank them for their dedication and sacrifice. We remember those who gave their lives for the cause of liberty on Memorial Day and observe Veterans Day to show honor to all who have served in the armed forces. Even Independence Day can be a treasured time to express gratitude to the men and women who pay such a dear price to ensure our country's freedom. Encouraging letters can also be a lifeline to soldiers who are stationed far from home.

WORDS OF THANKSGIVING

As autumn gilds foliage in burnished hues, let thoughts of gratitude scatter across hill and dale like fall leaves dancing on the breeze. Kind sentiments are often shared on Thanksgiving Day when family members gather for a feast, but these affirmations become even more dear when also preserved on paper. Write letters to relatives in the weeks leading up to the holiday, pen notes inside place cards, or let children at the gathering craft cornucopias of their most appreciated blessings.

HAPPY
HOLIDAYS
THE MEACHAMS
Dogwood Hill
M
WARMEST HOLIDAY WISHES
THE MEACHAM FAMILY
JON AND KEITH,
SAM, MARRY AND MAGGIE
2026
Dogwood Hill
M
KEITH MEACHAM

CHRISTMAS CARDS

One of the most time-honored traditions of Yuletide is the exchange of holiday greetings. Through the years, return addresses change, generations grow up and start families of their own, and many of life's most poignant transitions are chronicled in these beloved annual missives. Each year's Christmas card offers a sort of miniature time capsule, with the passing decades bringing about a cache of memories more valuable than any gift to be found beneath the tree.

ICTORIAL
LIFE OF
ASHINGTON
A MERRIE CHRISTMAS
A HAPPY

"GIFTS OF TIME AND
LOVE ARE SURELY THE
BASIC INGREDIENTS
OF A TRULY MERRY
CHRISTMAS."
—Peg Bracken

Showcasing Christmas cards allows the friendly salutations to add cheer throughout the season. In this charming bedroom, a garland of fresh greenery, magnolia clippings, and berries offers a fragrant backdrop for a beribboned display of glad tidings.

From

May your Brightest Xmas

Happy Year.

NAME

ADDRESS

407 North 6th St.

1949

NEAREST RELATIVE

NAME

407 North 6th St

ADDRESS

To

From

POP POP

Oct 4 1995

Not all postcards from the past come with a postmark; some connections to previous generations await in the familiar handwriting of a forebear whose diary, recipe box, photo album, or other heirloom opens a cache of prized memories.

ON *Keeping* A *Diary*

Journaling is a time of reflection treasured by many, but where should one begin in cultivating this practice? Simple yet timeless advice from William Wordsworth suggests, "Fill your paper with the breathings of your heart."

LE CAHIER
Nº01
DREAM
JOURNAL

TEXT GLENDA WINDERS

My reclusive neighbor, Mamie Shock, invited me into her home only once. On a winter's day, when I was shoveling snow off my sidewalk, she called across our white lawns that I needed to come in for a cup of tea. Unfortunately, she died soon after that, and another neighbor who had a key to her house gave me a tour. There was a butler's pantry, a marble fireplace, and a bathroom with a claw-foot tub, but none of these amenities charmed me like the shelves in the study that were filled with black spiral-bound notebooks.

I pulled one out at random and discovered they were Mamie's diaries—nearly fifty years of the details of her life: "The plumber came about the water heater"; "Invited the Nelsons to dinner." Writing down these events had infused her quiet days with meaning.

I started doing the same thing and using the same kind of book, but I added Abraham Lincoln's well-known quote to the first page: "We can complain because rose bushes have thorns, or rejoice because thorn bushes have roses"—a reminder to stay positive as each January begins.

My husband liked these chronicles because they were useful in a practical sense. When he wondered when we had last taken the car in for service, I could look it up. When my children wanted to know what pieces they had played at a certain piano recital, I could tell them.

After that marriage ended, I remarried and acquired a new mother-in-law who was fascinated with my habit, so I began giving her a diary every year for Christmas. She preferred books with pictures of flowers scattered throughout them and just a few lines for writing. "I don't think I'll have as much to write about as you do," she explained.

Her son (my husband) liked calling out a random date and having me read what I had written. "September 24, 2003," he'd say, and my note-taking would call to mind a time we would otherwise have forgotten.

When his mother died, he and his brothers gave her few journals to me, thinking it would be too painful for them to read what she had written. But I found this "bonus visit" with her to be delightful. As I perused the volumes one rainy afternoon, I realized she had gone in a different direction and had used them as an opportunity to plant love notes for her family to discover later on: "I'm so happy Jerry found such a lovely woman," she wrote. "Jack's girls are becoming so grown-up and pretty"; "Jim is doing so well at his new job."

That night, I started writing love notes to my family, too—not every day, but when they did something that touched me, I recorded it. After her first child was born, my daughter kept a diary in the same kind of black spiral-bound book I had been using. Her idea was to preserve the milestones of her children's lives by including such things as the first time they walked, got a new tooth, or had a birthday party. When they learned to talk, she kept a list of words they mispronounced to comic effect, such as "eskited" instead of "excited."

I duplicated her idea of keeping lists, but mine consist of New Year's resolutions I can refer to throughout the year and books I've read that I can recommend to friends. Noting the day's high and low at the bottom of the page was another of my daughter's innovations that I adopted. This compels me to reflect on each day in gratitude and reminds me how lucky I am when the fact that "the cable guy never showed up" is my "low."

When my daughter reached the age I was when I began my diaries, she asked if she could read the book I'd kept for that year. I said yes, hoping she would glean some wisdom from my experiences in the areas where her life has echoed mine—children, divorce, new love, and career.

Recently, my teenage granddaughter has begun keeping track of her life, too, and her addition is to spice up the entries with colorful inks and drawings. Today, we are three generations who look forward to opening our journals at the new year and wondering what adventures we will record, what ups and downs will frame our days, and what love notes we will write to the future.

Threads of CONNECTION

Combining the enjoyment of cross-stitching with the nostalgic appeal of redwork embroidery, canvases printed by former Artist-in-Residence Stephanie Monahan, also featured on page 46, evoke the charm of bygone days. Cotton filament in Turkey red gained popularity in nineteenth-century America for its colorfast nature and affordability. Employing increasingly intricate techniques, schoolgirls learned the way of the needle, along with fundamentals of reading and writing, and women explored infinite possibilities for adding bespoke embellishments to household objects from tea towels to quilts.

Reminiscent of antique tracery, old-fashioned motifs rendered on faux linen allow modern hobbyists to pursue a pastime tied to genteel female instruction, creativity, and edification. A primitive alphabet takes its inspiration from a marking sampler, which would have introduced a pupil to embroidery, while a simply adorned quote from Jane Austen extols the virtues of home. Wrought with a single strand of floss, each X offers a tangible link to cherished traditions.

Ah! There
is nothing
like staying
at home
for real
comfort

PAGES *Past*

Beyond the author's poetry or prose, an old book may convey other whispers from times gone by. An inscription inside the front cover tells the story of the first pair to find connection within the volume, while observations or illustrations scrawled in the margins of the text speak to the next reader to get lost in the pages.

TEXT E. M. CORSA

Thin slices of gold edge the velvety soft paper, delicate as lace and smelling of afternoon tea. The inscriptions are faded—some in pencil—lovingly addressed to grandchildren, parents, and friends. My fingertips trace the scripts, exquisitely crafted and dated, leaving me curious about the giver and the receiver.

I have always loved books—especially the old ones barely held together by their brittle skeletons and blemished cloth skins. Much care was taken in crafting the covers and selecting the artists to create the lush illustrations inside. As an artist myself, my favorite books are the poetry books from the 1800s published in England that, fortunately, made their way across the pond. These are the books where writers left their hearts on the page along with their ink. Pledges of love, heartache, joy, and contemplation are highlighted with flowers, landscapes, and portraits. The words may be dated, but the emotions remain the same no matter what the year. Many poems are about loss—of a love, a home, a parent, or a child—written while lifesaving medicine was still in its infancy. It's difficult for me to read these, especially the ones about children, being a mother myself.

Most of these books are themed around the seasons, sometimes half-full of summer with seaside images or half-empty with winter's snow and smoke from a chimney. Autumn brings the harvest of apples and pumpkins, and spring offers renewal with a bird's nest full of eggs nestled into the crook of a tree limb. But even in the darkest of winter's passages, there always seems to be a feeling of hope.

Women with fringed parasols share a hot summer day on one side of the page while fishermen bringing in the day's catch are revealed on the other side. Birds wing their way from sunrise through nightfall. Insects share the page with turtles, and love letters appear for girls and boys meeting alongside a brook or in a shady glade. There are fables to be told by the water lilies, who have witnessed an underwater flirtation of the hands while chaperones watch from above. And visitors to a garden seat share a poem and a page all on the same afternoon.

The foxing and yellowing, creasing, tiny holes, and tears on the pages don't bother me. They offer additional layers of texture and time. The poems and engravings partner with each other like arranged marriages destined for happiness and eternity. Like an arranged marriage, this kind of poetry is rare, not in fashion anymore. Yet all my senses are satiated; the sight of a perfect composition of the page, the sound of a poem being read aloud, the smell of the page itself, the touch on my fingers of the embossed cover boards, and the taste making its presence known in my hunger for more.

So when I see an old book, unraveling, torn and tossed aside, my heart aches. Scooping up the loose yellowing pages, I take them back to my studio, where I can sit and become intimately acquainted with each one, letting it tell me its story and suggest a subject for me to illustrate. I read the poet's words sometimes two or three times. I look at the reproduced engravings, marveling at the intricacy of each one, something I could never do myself. But I do have the ability to bring these pages back to life with colored pencils, watercolors, and a touch of fancy, with the hope that eventually they will find a home, and the lost words and illustrations can once again be enjoyed in a new format. These pages capture a moment past within the present.

One day, I will run out of antique pages as I will of time. Will anyone write a poem for me or paint a picture edged in gold to comfort those I love? How wonderful to be remembered.

The Poetry OF FLOWERS

Although plants have been imbued with symbolism for centuries, the nuanced art of "floriography" reached its peak during Victorian times. Still today, bouquets reflect our deepest sentiments—especially when they convey the language of flowers.

IN MY THOUGHTS

Lovely and bright, a pair of posies mirrors the soul-stirring sense of renewal kindled by hours spent in treasured company. Among verdant leaves of ivy and geranium—foliage placed to suggest an enduring connection—ranunculus, chrysanthemums, and roses echo the joy of esprit de corps.

WEDDED BLISS

Showcasing stephanotis for marital happiness, this arrangement balances softness and strength with baby's breath and gardenias for purity, and sweet William for gallantry. Ferns speak to the sincerity of marriage vows, while laurel, which will never wilt, signifies fidelity.

"FLOWERS HAVE A LANGUAGE THAT EVERYONE CAN UNDERSTAND— THE LANGUAGE OF BEAUTY AND LOVE."

—Debasish Mridha

Heirloom RECIPES

Love letters to past family gatherings, holiday menus, and everyday meals, recipe cards written in the hand of a beloved matriarch bring back memories, not only of favorite dishes but also of the love that went into their preparation.

Cherished GEMS

Collections of sparkling baubles, prized pieces of estate jewelry, monogrammed ring boxes, and other treasures of the jewelry chest offer glimmers of past relationships, tangible connections to previous generations, and notes on the wonders of human connection.

Ruth
Mommy

For collector Courtney Hildebrand, there is magic in a sterling ring box. The precious metal, which she's gathered for decades, is familiar to her, like the smile of an old friend. The stories each piece could share, however, are a mystery she constantly pursues.

"It looks like a piece of candy to me," Courtney says. She discovered the collectible in the pages of *Victoria* before procuring her first at a Memphis flea market. To this day, that initial find is her most precious. Manufactured by Birks, the standard-setter of Canadian jewelry, this 1930s antique was marked with a Royal Warrant of Appointment from the Prince of Wales—an indication of the royal family's patronage, which makes the box all the more valuable.

Most of Courtney's collection dates to the early twentieth century and hails from America, Canada, or England. When she searches, she aspires to curate variety among her pieces. They may be round, square, or heart-shaped, with a vibrant velvet or satin lining in shades of emerald, ruby, or even eggplant. The handcrafted interior indicates the care artisans took in creating each box long ago, as well as the love imbued by its owner over the many years since.

To protect the silver from tarnishing, Courtney advises collectors to enclose the boxes behind glass, as too much polishing can fade any engravings over time. These inscriptions are often the only way to verify the item's origin, though some pieces are unmarked, and others still were engraved for personal reasons long after their original use. Although much of the provenance of sterling ring boxes remains a mystery, Courtney fervently researches in libraries and online forums, aiming to spread her knowledge to antiques lovers around the world.

Mary

POST
MANVS
EVS qui humanæ
tatem mirabiliter
noſtræ
Ieſus Chriſtus
noſter. Qui tecum.

BRILLIANCE OF BIRTHSTONES

There are myriad ways to incorporate birthstones into a jewelry collection, from an aquamarine bracelet for those born in March to amethyst and tanzanite treasures for February and December birthdays, respectively. Lucky ladies who arrived in April can claim diamonds as their own special gem, while November captures the warmth of citrine and topaz. For a special keepsake, a mother can combine the birthstones of her children to create a one-of-a-kind piece.

Mom would have been 101
this Feb. So she was
probably ! yr. in the picture

FROM A DIFFERENT TIME AND PLACE

Among some of the most fascinating ephemera to discover are musings penned long ago in personal letters. Collectors find endless delight in rereading accounts of lives lived out long ago or far away. But even details jotted onto the backs of weathered photographs can be viewed as correspondence, with names and dates drawing posterity into moments worthy of remembrance. May the words we leave behind serve as love notes to generations to come.

CREDITS & RESOURCES

Editor: Melissa Lester
Senior Director of Design:
Melissa Sturdivant Smith
Associate Editors:
Kassidy Abernathy, Leslie Bennett Smith
Assistant Editor: Lydia McMullen
Administrative Senior Art Director:
Tracy Wood-Franklin
Editorial Assistant: Audra Shalles
Senior Copy Editor: Meg Lundberg
Copy Editor: Michele Moore
Senior Digital Imaging Specialist: Delisa McDaniel

CONTRIBUTING WRITERS

MARIE BAXLEY: page 62
KAREN CALLAWAY: pages 30–34, 66–81, and 159
POLLY CAMPBELL: page 38
AMY CATES: page 57
E. M. CORSA: page 145
KATHLEEN THOMPSON: pages 22–25
GLENDA WINDERS: page 141

CONTRIBUTING PHOTOGRAPHERS

KIMBERLY FINKEL DAVIS: pages 38–39, 56–57, and 106
KRISTINE FOLEY: page 161
JANE HOPE: pages 41 and 66–67, 69–75, and 78–79
GEORGIANA LANE: pages 23 and 124
MAC JAMIESON: pages 2, 10, 12–15, 24, 40, 43, 46–48, 54–55, 82, 101, 103, 105, 114–116, 120, 128, 131, 140, 142–144, 146–151, 153–157, and 160
JOHN O'HAGAN: pages 62–63 and 161
KATE SEARS: pages 76–77, 80–81, and 106–107
MARCY BLACK SIMPSON: cover and pages 6–8, 16–22, 25, 34–37, 44, 50–51, 64, 86–87, 96–98, 100, 102, 104, 106, 109–110, 121, 125–126, 138–139, 152, and 158–159
STEPHANIE WELBOURNE STEELE: pages 4–5, 22, 26, 28–33, 40, 42, 44–45, 49, 52, 58–61, 108, 111–113, 118, 119–120, 122–123, 126–127, 129–130, 132–136, and 161

CONTRIBUTING STLYISTS

SIDNEY BRAGIEL: cover and pages 4–8, 10, 16–21, 44, 49, 52–64, 82, 86–87, 91–95, 98, 114–115, 131–132, 136, 152, and 160
MISSIE NEVILLE CRAWFORD: page 25
YUKIE MCLEAN: page 106
JORDAN MARXER MILLNER: page 139
TERESA H. SABANKAYA: pages 86–87
MELISSA STURDIVANT SMITH: pages 2, 12–15, 22, 24, 26, 28–34, 40, 42–45, 48, 52, 96–97, 116, 118–123, 125–131, 134–135, 138, 140, 144, 146–151, 153–156, 158–159, and 161

WHERE TO SHOP & BUY

Below is a listing of products and companies featured in this book.

Cover and pages 6–8, 16–21, 52, 54, 64, 91, and 98: Special thanks to Kathryn Hastings & Co., @kathrynhastingsco on Instagram, kathrynhastingsco.com.
Page 2: Pandora de Balthazár Fine Linens, 418 East Wright Street, Pensacola, FL, pandoradebalthazar.com.
Page 10: Every Little Something: Foil-Metallic Blue Merci Stationery Scalloped, Foil-Metallic Gold Merci Stationery Scalloped; everylittlesomething.com.
Page 12: Herend: Princess Victoria Green Tea Pot with Rose; herendusa.com.
Pages 12–14, 146–151, and 158–159: Special thanks to Maison de France Antiques, 1304 8th Street, Leeds, AL, 205-699-6330.
Page 23: Special thanks to Corey Amaro, stylist and lifestyle blogger, coreyamaro@aol.com, willows95988.typepad.com.
Page 23: Haute Papier: custom stationery wardrobe; hautepapier.com.
Page 24: For more of Riley Sheehey's artwork, visit her website, rileysheehey.com.
Pages 25, 46–47, and 142–143: To explore artisan Stephanie Monahan's wares, visit her website at monahanpapers.com.
Pages 26, 29, and 32: Marchioness Home & Garden, info@marchioness.com, marchioness .com. WOMA Design, womadesign.com.
Pages 28 and 31–32: Jennifer Reynolds Calligraphy, @jenniferreynolds.calligraphy on Instagram.
Pages 30 and 32: Papira Design + Letterpress: IN164 Suite; papira.ro.
Pages 30–32: Prints Charming Soho, 1903 Cahaba Road, Mountain Brook, AL, @printscharmingsohonyc on Instagram, printscharmingsoho.com.
Pages 31 and 33: The Wells Makery, thewellsmakery.com.
Page 34: Illustrations by Julie of @manonboudoir on Instagram, manonboudoir.com.
Pages 34–37: Hôtel Caron de Beaumarchais, 12 Rue Vieille-du-Temple, 75004 Paris, France, carondebeaumarchais.com.
Page 40: Bell'Invito: Love Monogram Desk Sheet Set, Gold Crown Stationery, Engraved and Letterpress Bird & Branch Social Notes; bellinvito.com. Casa Felix: Al Fresco Stationery; hello@casafelix.com, casafelix.com. Carolina Elizabeth: Roses in Blown Glass, Cabbage Rose in Blue and White, Old English Roses on Linen, Roses in Silver with Tangerine; carolinaelizabeth. com. Writer's Hammer: Gear Shift Themed Pen; etsy.com/shop/writershammer.
Page 41: Columbia Road, London, England; columbiaroad.info.
Page 42: Maileg: Blue Bird Gift Wrap; mailegusa.com. Odd Balls: Bunch of Blooms Folded Note, Canton Collection Invitation, China Blue Placecard, Chinese Green Ribboned Invitation, Lacecap Blue Invitation, Topiary Response Card; oddballsinvitations.net.
Page 44: Authentic Models: Campaign Lap Desk & Writing Set, authenticmodels.com. Arpa: Arpa Correspondence Sheet & Policy Envelope in Ivory, Arpa Social Note Set in Pale Blue; Récife: Rollerball Pen in Vanilla; from Orange Art, orangeartstore.com. Royal Crown Derby: Footed Cup & Saucer Set in Gold Aves; from Replacements, Ltdreplacements.com.
Pages 44–45 and 161: Special thanks to Adams Antiques & The Potager, adamsantiquesandthepotager.com.
Pages 45 and 146–151: Special thanks to Tricia's Treasures, 205-871-9779, triciastreasures.us.
Pages 50–51: Hills & Dales Estate, 1916 Hills and Dales Drive, LaGrange, GA, hillsanddales.org.
Page 52: Assorted pens from Bromberg's, brombergs.com.
Pages 52 and 58: Vintage letters from Prints Charming Soho, printscharmingsoho.com.
Pages 54–55: Explore more of Marsha Lassiter's calligraphy by following @marshalassitercalligraphy on Instagram.
Page 54: Kathryn Hastings & Co.: Wax Seal; kathrynhastingsco.com. Marbled Paper Studio: Marbled Stationery; marbledpaperstudio @yahoo.com, marbledpaperstudio.com.
Page 59: Waterford Crystal: Lismore Letter Opener with Stainless Blade; Royal Copenhagen: Letter Opener & Box-Ononis spinosa Mull Flora Danica; Reed & Barton: Letter Opener with Stainless Blade Francis I; from Replacements, Ltd., replacements.com.
Pages 62–63: Assorted calling cards; Surcie, shopsurcie.com; Key Circle Press, keycirclepress .com; Jennifer Reynolds Calligraphy, jenniferreynoldscalligraphy@gmail.com, @jenniferreynolds.calligraphy on Instagram; and Paper Eliza, papereliza.com.
Pages 66–67: Jane Austen Centre, 40 Gay Street, Bath, United Kingdom, BA1 2NT, janeausten.co.uk. Jane Austen's House Museum, Winchester Road,

Chawton, Hampshire GU34 1SD, janeaustens.house.
Pages 68–69: Brontë Parsonage Museum, Church Street, Haworth, West Yorkshire, BD22 8DR, United Kingdom, bronte.org.uk.
Pages 70–71: Newstead Abbey, Ravenshead, Nottinghamshire, NG15 9HJ, United Kingdom, newsteadabbey.org.uk.
Pages 72–73: The Kilns, Headington, Oxford, OX3 8JD, United Kingdom, thekilns@cslewis.org, cslewis.org/ourprograms/thekilns. C. S. Lewis Foundation, 301 9th Street #206, Redlands, CA, cslewis.org.
Pages 74–75: Keats House, 10 Keats Grove, London, NW3 2RR, United Kingdom, cityoflondon.gov.uk.
Pages 76–77: For more information on Beatrix Potter, visit golakes.co.uk, nationaltrust.org.uk, and yewtree-farm.com.
Pages 78–79: The Bloomsbury Hotel, 16–22 Great Russell Street, London, WC1B 3NN, United Kingdom, doylecollection.com/hotels/the-bloomsbury-hotel.
Pages 80–81: Rydal Mount, Ambleside, Lake District, LA22 9LU, United Kingdom, rydalmount.co.uk.
Page 82: Marbled Paper Studio: Marbled envelope; marbledpaperstudio@yahoo.com, marbledpaperstudio.com.
Pages 84–85: Bilancia Designs: gift tags, calligraphed note card; bilanciadesigns.com. Marbled Paper Studio: marbled notecard and ribbon, marbled stationery; marbledpaperstudio@yahoo.com, marbledpaperstudio.com.
Page 85: LouLou Baker: stationery set; louloubaker.com.
Pages 86–87: To see more of Teresa Sabankaya's work, visit teresasabankaya.com.
Page 88: Bilancia Designs: Calligraphy tag with dried florals; bilanciadesigns.com.
Page 89: Bilancia Designs: Calligraphy tag; bilanciadesigns.com. Marbled Paper Studio: ribbons, wax seals; marbledpaperstudio@yahoo.com, marbledpaperstudio.com.
Page 90: Key Circle Press: Baptism invitation; kathleen@keycirclepress.com, keycirclepress.com.
Page 91: Assorted invitations; Dogwood Hill, support@dogwood-hill.com, dogwood-hill.com. Empress Stationery, empressstationery.com.
Page 92: Bilancia Designs: gift tag; bilanciadesigns.com.
Page 93: Dogwood Hill: Heron Green Wedding Collection; support@dogwood-hill.com, dogwood-hill.com. Marbled Paper Studio: Marbled card and envelope; marbledpaperstudio@yahoo.com, marbledpaperstudio.com.
Page 94: Dogwood Hill: Save the Date card; support@dogwood-hill.com, dogwood-hill.com. Key Circle Press: Save the Date card, We've Moved card; kathleen@keycirclepress.com, keycirclepress.com.
Page 95: Key Circle Press: Baby Announcement card; kathleen@keycirclepress.com, keycirclepress.com.
Pages 96–97: Kim Seybert: Frost Placemat in blush, Herringbone Napkin in white, gold, and silver; kimseybert.com. Moser: Royal Champagne Flute; moser.com. Oneida: Golden Michelangelo 5-Piece Fine Place Setting; oneida.com. Sasha Nicholas: Custom "V" with Crown Salad Plate; sashanicholas.com. Special thanks to Kim Cobb of Flying Squirrel Cookies, flyingsquirrelcookies@gmail.com; PRE Event Resources, 1209 James Harrison Jr. Parkway, Tuscaloosa, AL; Reliant, reliantribbon.com; Empress Stationery; empressstationery.com.
Pages 100, 102, and 104: Nancy Hopkins Handlettering, nancy@hopkinslettering.com, hopkinslettering.com.
Pages 101, 103, and 105: Allison R. Banks Designs: custom monogramming and calligraphy; allisonrbanksdesigns.com
Page 106: Wendy Addison, 11 Canyon Lake Drive, Port Costa, CA, wendyaddisonstudio.com. Wiley Valentine, 17891 Sky Park Circle, Suite B, Irvine, California, wileyvalentine.com.
Pages 106–107: Austin Press, austinpress.com.
Pages 108–111: Paula Skene Designs, paulaskenedesigns.com.
Pages 112–113: Dollhouse and Toy Museum of Vermont, 212 Union Street, Bennington, VT, dollhouseandtoymuseumofvermont.com.
Pages 114–115: ExVoto, 2416 Canterbury Road, Birmingham, AL, exvotovintage.com. Jennifer Reynolds Calligraphy, jenniferreynoldscalligraphy@gmail.com, @jenniferreynolds.calligraphy on Instagram.
Pages 116 and 120: Special thanks to Maribel Polanco of White Berry Lane, @whiteberrylane on Instagram.
Page 118: Oblation Papers & Press: Handmade Paper in Blush, Traveler's Company Brass Fountain Pen, Letter Sheets with Holly Sprig, Pocket Journal Thoughts; oblationpapers.com.
Page 119: Haute Papier: Custom stationery wardrobe; hautepapier.com. Oblation Papers & Press: Many Thanks, Petite Cream Deckled Heart; oblationpapers.com.
Page 120: Royal Albert: Lady Carlyle Teapot & Lid, Lady Carlyle Sugar Bowl & Lid; from Replacements, Ltd., replacements.com. Royal Albert: 100 Years of Royal Albert 1960 Golden Rose 3-Piece Place Setting; from Wedgwood, wedgwood com.
Page 121: D. Blümchen & Company: Valentine Cupid Postcards; blumchen.com.
Page 123: East Coast Trimming: antique ribbon; eastcoasttrimming.com. JRD Art Shop: Styling surfaces, jrdartshop.com. The Vintage Inkwell: custom paper goods; hello@thevintageinkwell.com, thevintageinkwell.com. Trumpet and Horn: vintage and vintage-inspired rings; trumpetandhorn.com.
Page 127: Casa Felix: Al Fresco Stationery; hello@casafelix.com, casafelix.com. Demuth Yellow and Blue Watercolor Scarf; store.metmuseum.org.
Page 128: The Muddy Dog: Patriotic Tote Folded Notecard, Nantucket Basket Folded Notecard, Luxury Land of The Free Folded Notecard; themuddydog.com.
Page 129: Camilla Moss: hand-painted Thanksgiving stationery ; camillamoss.com.
Page 130: Dogwood Hill: Keith Meacham Crest Collection; support@dogwood-hill.com, dogwood-hill.com.
Page 131: Dogwood Hill: Green Flora Bow Wrapping Paper Roll by Dogwood Hill, Green Flora Bow Gift Tags by Inslee Fariss; support@dogwood-hill.com, dogwood-hill.com.
Pages 132–133: The Brittany House Antiques at Oak Hill, 5931 AL-21, Oak Hill, AL, thebrittanyhouseantiquesatoakhill.com.
Page 139: Special thanks to Shannon and Wlady Grochowski of Le Châtelaine Chocolat Co., 110 South Rouse Avenue, Bozeman, MT, chatelainechocolate.com. French Countryside Companion, frenchcountrysidecompanion.com.
Page 140: Every Little Something: Foil-Pastel Blue Merci Stationery Set, Delft Blue Stationery Set; everylittlesomething.com. Papier: Le Moderne Foiled Notebook in Vintage Blue, Antique Blue Notebook; papier.com. Robed With Love: Waverly Sleep Mask; heretohelp@ robedwithlove.com, robedwithlove.com.
Pages 142–143: For more information about needlework reproductionist Vickie LoPiccolo Jennett, visit her website at needleworkpress.com.
Page 153: Royal Copenhagen: Blue Fluted Plain Flat Cup & Saucer Set, Mega Blue Fluted Tea Pot & Lid, Blue Fluted Half Lace Border Jug; from Replacements, Ltd., replacements.com.
Pages 154–156: Special thanks to Courtney Hildebrand. Learn more about her collection at ringboxesgalore.net.
Pages 158–159: Van Atkins Jewelers, 129 West Bankhead Street, New Albany, MS, vanatkins.com.

"LET YOUR PEN FAITHFULLY REFLECT THE GLINT OF LIGHT FROM YOUR SOUL."

—Terri Guillemets